D1613904

THIS COLORING BOOK BELONGS TO:

_____

_____

_____

_____

_____

JESUS

THE TRUE MEANING OF EASTER IS TO REMEMBER JESUS CHRIST'S CRUCIFIXION, AND CELEBRATE HIS RESURRECTION. WHEN JESUS ENTERED THE CITY OF JERUSALEM, HE RODE ON A DONKEY WHILE PEOPLE IN THE STREET WAVED PALM LEAVES. IN ANCIENT TIMES A PALM LEAF SYMBOLIZED VICTORY AND PEACE. THE PEOPLE WAVED PALM LEAVES AS JESUS ARRIVED BECAUSE THEY KNEW HE WAS THE SAVIOR OF THE WORLD.

THE LAST SUPPER

JESUS KNEW THAT HE WOULD SOON BE KILLED, SO HE GATHERED HIS DISCIPLES TOGETHER TO HAVE ONE LAST MEAL WITH THEM. HE TAUGHT THEM ABOUT THE SACRAMENT. HE GAVE THE DISCIPLES BREAD TO REPRESENT HIS BODY AND WINE TO REPRESENT HIS BLOOD. JESUS USED THIS SYMBOLISM TO TALK TO HIS FOLLOWERS ABOUT THE SACRIFICE HE WOULD MAKE TO REDEEM ALL MANKIND.

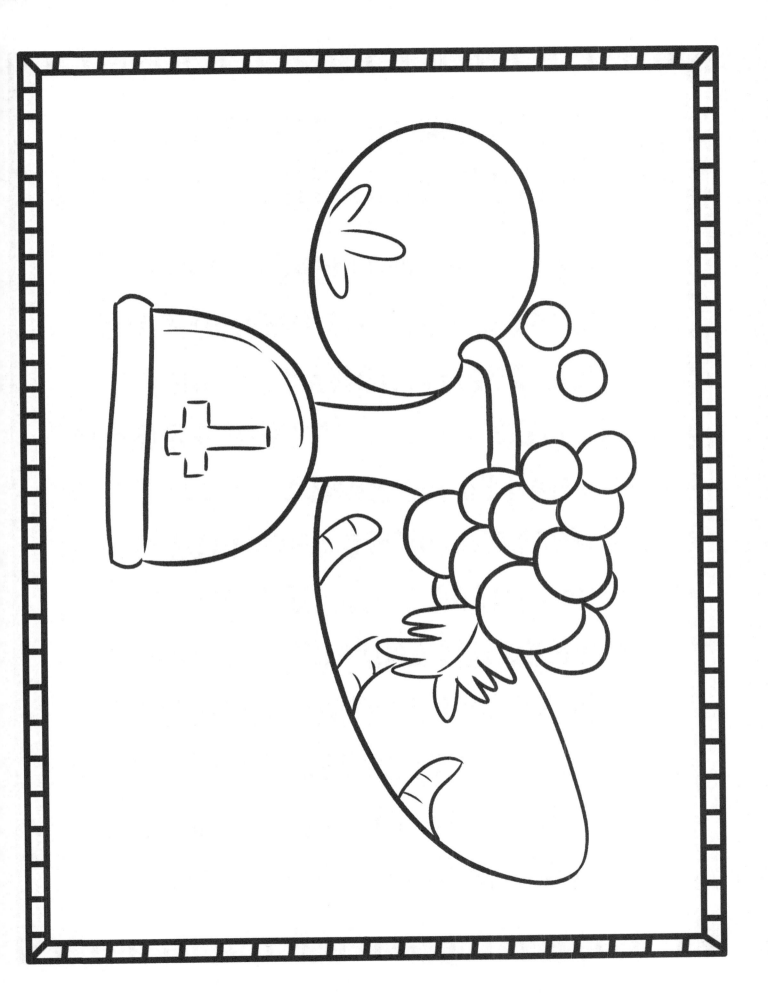

CRUCIFIXION

A GROUP OF UNBELIEVERS FALSELY ACCUSED JESUS OF TREASON AND BLASPHEMY. ROMAN SOLDIERS ARRESTED JESUS AND CRUCIFIED HIM. THEY NAILED HIS HANDS AND FEET TO A WOODEN CROSS AND MADE HIM HANG THERE UNTIL HE DIED. THEY MOCKED HIM AND PUT A CROWN OF THORNS ON HIS HEAD. WHEN JESUS DIED ON THE CROSS THE SKIES DARKENED AND EARTHQUAKES, FIRES, AND GREAT WINDS RAGED.

THE TOMB

AFTER JESUS DIED HIS DISCIPLES TOOK HIS BODY AND LAID IT IN A TOMB. THEY CLEANED HIS BODY AND WRAPPED IT IN WHITE LINEN. HIS FRIENDS WERE AFRAID THAT BAD PEOPLE WOULD TRY TO STEAL OR HARM JESUS' BODY, SO THEY ROLLED A LARGE STONE IN FRONT OF THE OPENING OF HIS TOMB. THEY ALSO HAD A GUARD STAND IN FRONT OF HIS TOMB TO PROTECT IT.

MARY MAGDALENE

THREE DAYS AFTER JESUS' DEATH MARY MAGDALENE WENT TO HIS TOMB. SHE DISCOVERED THAT THE STONE MEANT TO PROTECT THE TOMB HAD BEEN ROLLED AWAY, AND WHEN SHE ENTERED THE TOMB SHE FOUND THAT THE BODY OF JESUS WAS NO LONGER THERE. SHE WEPT, THINKING THAT SOMEONE HAD STOLEN CHRIST'S BODY.

RESURRECTION

A MAN APPROACHED MARY AND ASKED HER WHY SHE WAS CRYING. SHE TOLD THE MAN THAT SOMEONE HAD TAKEN THE BODY OF THE SAVIOR AND SHE DIDN'T KNOW WHERE. THEN WHEN MARY TURNED AROUND SHE SAW THAT THE MAN WAS JESUS CHRIST. HE HAD RISEN FROM THE DEAD!

EASTER NOW

WHAT EASTER TRADITIONS DO YOU ENJOY? WHILE WE SHOULD ALWAYS REMEMBER JESUS DURING EASTER TIME, WE CAN ALSO ENJOY THE MANY FUN TRADITIONS OF THE HOLIDAY. LET'S LEARN MORE ABOUT THE EASTER TRADITIONS WE ENJOY TODAY!

SPRING

EASTER IS ALWAYS IN THE MONTH OF APRIL AND DURING THE SPRINGTIME. SPRING IS THE SEASON AFTER WINTER. AS THE WEATHER BEGINS TO WARM AND SNOW MELTS AWAY, MANY ANIMALS BEGIN TO HAVE THEIR BABIES, AND FLOWERS BEGIN TO BLOOM. IN THE SPRINGTIME YOU CAN SEE BABY CHICKS HATCH FROM THEIR EGGS, OR BUTTERFLIES EMERGING FROM THEIR COCOONS. SPRING IS THE SEASON OF NEW LIFE, WHICH IS ONE OF THE REASONS WE CELEBRATE CHRIST'S RESURRECTION DURING THIS TIME.

EASTER EGGS

HAVE YOU EVER PAINTED AN EASTER EGG, OR GONE ON AN EASTER EGG HUNT? IN ANCIENT TIMES AN EGG WAS A SYMBOL OF NEW LIFE, SINCE SOME BABY ANIMALS HATCH FROM EGGS. THEY ALSO SYMBOLIZE THE TOMB THAT CHRIST BROKE FREE FROM WHEN HE WAS RESURRECTED.

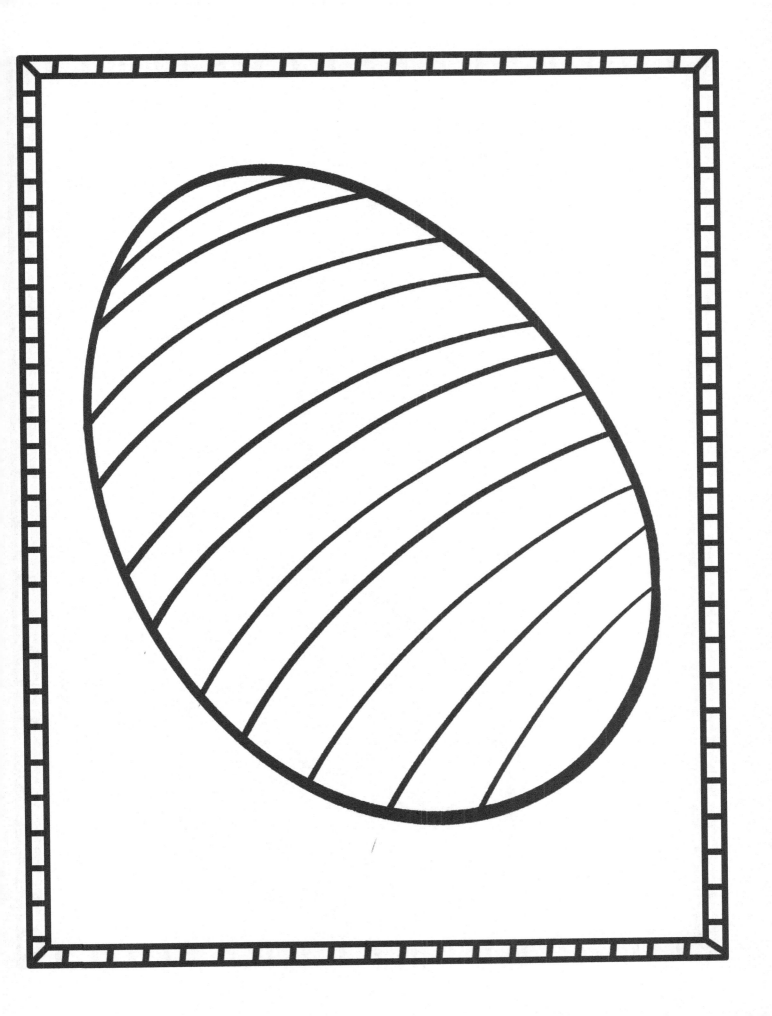

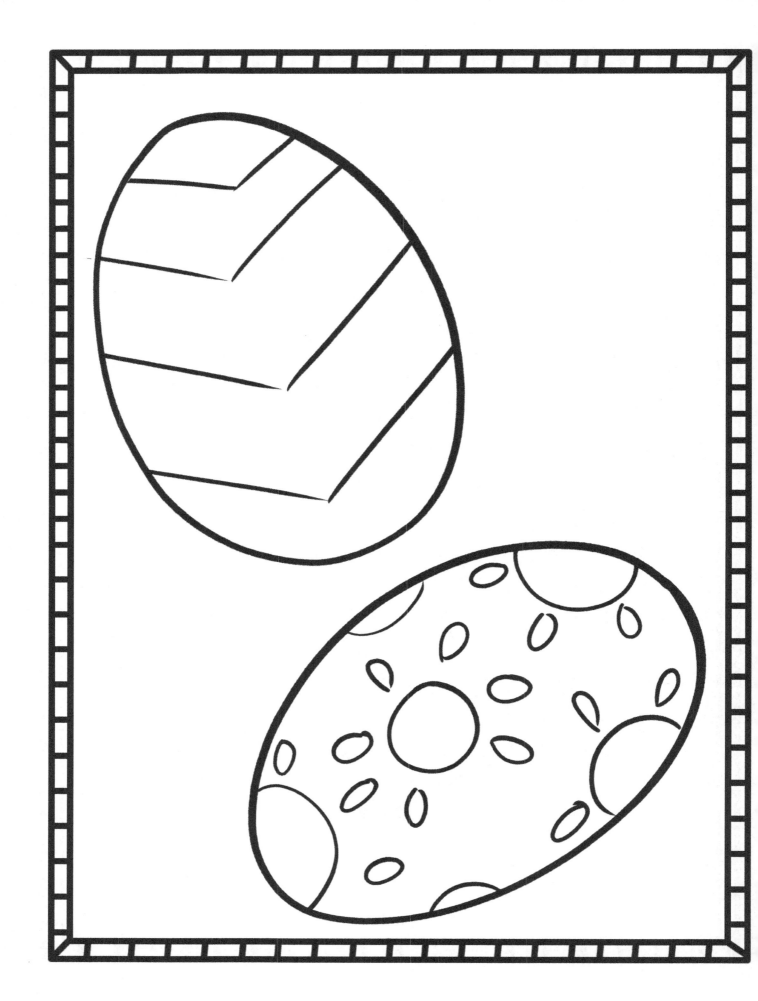

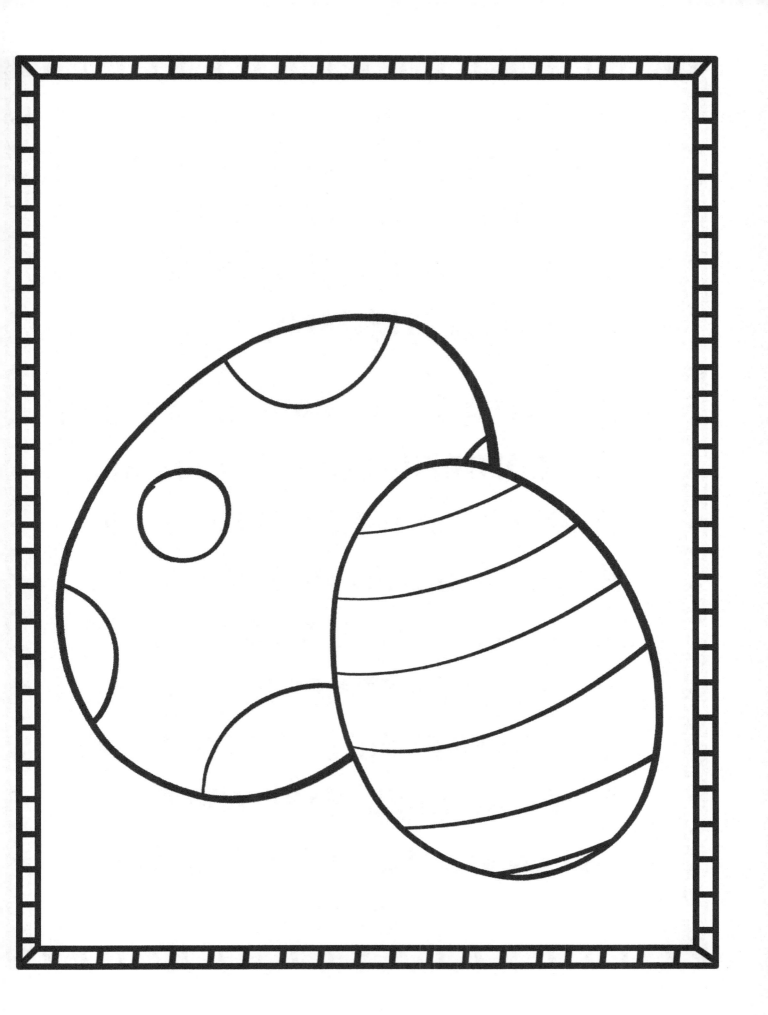

EASTER BUNNY

THE EASTER BUNNY BRINGS BASKETS AND COLORFUL EGGS TO KIDS ALL AROUND THE WORLD ON EASTER MORNING. SOMETIMES HE'LL HIDE EGGS OR PRIZES FOR YOU TO HUNT FOR, AND SOMETIMES HE'LL BRING YOU A BASKET FULL OF CANDY AND OTHER GOODIES. HAVE YOU EVER BEEN VISITED BY THE EASTER BUNNY?

Thank you for your purchase!

If you are happy with this book, please consider leaving a positive review on Amazon.com. Email us at learningbyprints@gmail.com with a screenshot of your 5 star review and you'll receive a free little gift as a thank you!

You may also like...

Learning By Prints

Find more fun and educational activities for your kids at www.learningbyprints.com

Made in the USA
Las Vegas, NV
01 April 2022

46682211R00024